Dedications

To my sons, Marquize C. Lovejoy and Caleb Lovejoy. I thank God for the men you have become. Thank you for always believing in me.

To Carita Montgomery – Thank you for your unwavering friendship and support. You continuously inspire me to do great things.

See your life change for the better!

I AM

30-Day Affirmation Challenge

Paytra Lovejoy

I AM: 30-Day Affirmation Challenge

Copyright © 2016 by Paytra Lovejoy

All rights reserved. Printed in the United States of America. No part of this book may be used or reproduced in any manner whatsoever without written permission except in the case of brief quotations embodied in critical articles or reviews.

For booking the author contact:
Paytra Lovejoy
4024 East Lake Pkwy
McDonough, GA 30253
www.PaytraLovejoy.com

For publisher information contact:
Claxco Publishers
950 Eagles Landing Pkwy #263
Stockbridge, GA 30281
www.GoClaxco.com

Book Editing, Layout, and Cover design by Claxco, LLC.
ISBN-Paperback: 978-0-9827738-5-7
First Edition: September 2016

10 9 8 7 6 5 4 3 2 1

Introduction

This book is a collection of daily declarations to speak over your life.

Whatever you release into the atmosphere of your environment—whether positive or negative—those words take action to become the driving forces of your success or failure.

Each day contains a theme word, along with its definition, and a statement to declare. After reading the definition, state the declaration four times. Then, take a moment to write your thoughts and feelings in response to your declaration. Anytime you write the vision, it becomes clearer and stronger, bringing alignment to your declaration.

After a few days, you will begin to see a positive change in your life's energy and direction.

I'm sure you will find a new source of identity as you frame your words with these "I Am" statements.

I want to stay connected with you beyond this book. That's why I'm giving away free resources to keep you motivated and inspired throughout your life. So, be sure to register your book on my website at www.PaytraLovejoy.com to stay up to date with the latest videos, downloads, and more.

You are becoming the person you speak into existence. I wish you the best in life.

- Paytra Lovejoy

Day 1

Today's Word:
Abundantly

Definition:

In large quantities, plentifully

Declaration:

I am "Abundantly" blessed

I am "Abundantly" blessed

I am "Abundantly" blessed

I am "Abundantly" blessed

"Write the vision, and make it plain upon tables, that he may run that readeth it."

- Habakkuk 2:2

Day 2

Today's Word:
Accomplished

Definition:

Highly trained or skilled

Declaration:

I am "Accomplished"

I am "Accomplished"

I am "Accomplished"

I am "Accomplished"

"Write the vision, and make it plain upon tables, that he may run that readeth it."

- Habakkuk 2:2

_____

_____

_____

_____

_____

_____

_____

_____

_____

_____

_____

_____

_____

Day 3

Today's Word:

Love

Definition:

An intense feeling of deep affection

Declaration:

I am "Love"

I am "Love"

I am "Love"

I am "Love"

"Write the vision, and make it plain upon tables, that he may run that readeth it."

- Habakkuk 2:2

_____

_____

_____

_____

_____

_____

_____

_____

_____

_____

_____

_____

Day 4

Today's Word:

Devoted

Definition:

Very loving or loyal

Declaration:

I am "Devoted"

I am "Devoted"

I am "Devoted"

I am "Devoted"

"Write the vision, and make it plain upon tables, that he may run that readeth it."

- Habakkuk 2:2

Day 5

Today's Word:
Peace

Definition:

Freedom from disturbance, quiet and tranquility

Declaration:

I am "Peace"

I am "Peace"

I am "Peace"

I am "Peace"

"Write the vision, and make it plain upon tables, that he may run that readeth it."

- Habakkuk 2:2

_____

_____

_____

_____

_____

_____

_____

_____

_____

_____

_____

Day 6

Today's Word:
Focused

Definition:

A central point, as of attraction, attention, or activity

Declaration:

I am "Focused"

I am "Focused"

I am "Focused"

I am "Focused"

"Write the vision, and make it plain upon tables, that he may run that readeth it."

- Habakkuk 2:2

Day 7

Today's Word:

Patient

Definition:

The capacity to accept or tolerate delay, problems, or suffering without getting annoyed or upset

Declaration:

I am "Patient"

I am "Patient"

I am "Patient"

I am "Patient"

"Write the vision, and make it plain upon tables, that he may run that readeth it."

- Habakkuk 2:2

Day 8

Today's Word:
Committed

Definition:

Feeling dedication and loyalty to a cause, activity, or job; wholeheartedly dedicated!

Declaration:

I am "Committed"

I am "Committed"

I am "Committed"

I am "Committed"

"Write the vision, and make it plain upon tables, that he may run that readeth it."

- Habakkuk 2:2

_____

_____

_____

_____

_____

_____

_____

_____

_____

_____

_____

_____

Day 9

Today's Word:
Different

Definition:

Not the same as another or each other,
unlike in nature, form or quality

Declaration:

I am "Different"

I am "Different"

I am "Different"

I am "Different"

"Write the vision, and make it plain upon tables, that he may run that readeth it."

- Habakkuk 2:2

_____

_____

_____

_____

_____

_____

_____

_____

_____

_____

_____

_____

Day 10

Today's Word:

Grateful

Definition:

Feeling or showing an appreciation of kindness, thankful

Declaration:

I am "Grateful"

I am "Grateful"

I am "Grateful"

I am "Grateful"

"Write the vision, and make it plain upon tables, that he may run that readeth it."

- Habakkuk 2:2

Day 11

Today's Word:
Proud

Definition:

Feeling deep pleasure or satisfaction as a result of one's own achievements

Declaration:

I am "Proud" of <u>MYSELF</u>

I am "Proud" of <u>MYSELF</u>

I am "Proud" of <u>MYSELF</u>

I am "Proud" of <u>MYSELF</u>

"Write the vision, and make it plain upon tables, that he may run that readeth it."

- Habakkuk 2:2

Day 12

Today's Word:
Wealthy

Definition:

Having a great deal of money, resources, or assets. Rich.

Declaration:

I am "Wealthy"

I am "Wealthy"

I am "Wealthy"

I am "Wealthy"

"Write the vision, and make it plain upon tables, that he may run that readeth it."

- Habakkuk 2:2

Day 13

Today's Word:

Positive

Definition:

A good alternative, or constructive quality or attribute

Declaration:

I am "Positive"

I am "Positive"

I am "Positive"

I am "Positive"

"Write the vision, and make it plain upon tables, that he may run that readeth it."

- Habakkuk 2:2

Day 14

Today's Word:
Important

Definition:
Of great significance or value likely to have a profound effect on success, survival on well being

Declaration:

I am "Important"

I am "Important"

I am "Important"

I am "Important"

"Write the vision, and make it plain upon tables, that he may run that readeth it."

- Habakkuk 2:2

_____

_____

_____

_____

_____

_____

_____

_____

_____

_____

_____

_____

_____

_____

Day 15

Today's Word:

Forgiving

Definition:

Ready and willing to forgive

Declaration:

I am "Forgiving"

I am "Forgiving"

I am "Forgiving"

I am "Forgiving"

"Write the vision, and make it plain upon tables, that he may run that readeth it."

- Habakkuk 2:2

Day 16

Today's Theme:

FROG

Meaning:

"Fully Relying on God"

Declaration:

I am "FROG"

I am "FROG"

I am "FROG"

I am "FROG"

"Write the vision, and make it plain upon tables, that he may run that readeth it."

- Habakkuk 2:2

_____

_____

_____

_____

_____

_____

_____

_____

_____

_____

_____

_____

Day 17

Today's Word:

Life

Definition:

The existence of an individual human being or animal

Declaration:

I am "Life"

I am "Life"

I am "Life"

I am "Life"

"Write the vision, and make it plain upon tables, that he may run that readeth it."

- Habakkuk 2:2

Day 18

Today's Word:

Millionaire

Definition:

A person whose assets are worth one million dollars or more

Declaration:

I am a "Millionaire"

I am a "Millionaire"

I am a "Millionaire"

I am a "Millionaire"

"Write the vision, and make it plain upon tables, that he may run that readeth it."

- Habakkuk 2:2

_____

_____

_____

_____

_____

_____

_____

_____

_____

_____

_____

_____

_____

Day 19

Today's Word:

Proactive

Definition:

Creativity or controlling a situation by causing something to happen rather than responding to it after it has happened

Declaration:

I am "Proactive"

I am "Proactive"

I am "Proactive"

I am "Proactive"

"Write the vision, and make it plain upon tables, that he may run that readeth it."

- Habakkuk 2:2

_____

_____

_____

_____

_____

_____

_____

_____

_____

_____

_____

_____

_____

Day 20

Today's Word:

Connected to God

Definition:

Having a divine connection

Declaration:

I am "Connected to God"

I am "Connected to God"

I am "Connected to God"

I am "Connected to God"

"Write the vision, and make it plain upon tables, that he may run that readeth it."

- Habakkuk 2:2

_____

_____

_____

_____

_____

_____

_____

_____

_____

_____

_____

_____

Day 21

Today's Word:

Success

Definition:

The accomplishment of an aim or purpose

Declaration:

I am "Success"

I am "Success"

I am "Success"

I am "Success"

"Write the vision, and make it plain upon tables, that he may run that readeth it."

- Habakkuk 2:2

Day 22

Today's Word:

Healthy

Definition:

To be in good health

Declaration:

I am "Healthy"

I am "Healthy"

I am "Healthy"

I am "Healthy"

"Write the vision, and make it plain upon tables, that he may run that readeth it."

- Habakkuk 2:2

Day 23

Today's Word:

Beautiful

Definition:

Of a very high standard, excellent

Declaration:

I am "Beautiful"

I am "Beautiful"

I am "Beautiful"

I am "Beautiful"

"Write the vision, and make it plain upon tables, that he may run that readeth it."

- Habakkuk 2:2

Day 24

Today's Word:

Divine

Definition:

Excellent, delightful

Declaration:

I am "Divine"

I am "Divine"

I am "Divine"

I am "Divine"

"Write the vision, and make it plain upon tables, that he may run that readeth it."

- Habakkuk 2:2

Day 25

Today's Word:

One

Definition:

Enough of (particular thing)

Declaration:

I am "One"

I am "One"

I am "One"

I am "One"

"Write the vision, and make it plain upon tables, that he may run that readeth it."

- Habakkuk 2:2

Day 26

Today's Word:

Unified

Definition:

Made one, united

Declaration:

I am "Unified with the Universe"

I am "Unified with the Universe"

I am "Unified with the Universe"

I am "Unified with the Universe"

"Write the vision, and make it plain upon tables, that he may run that readeth it."

- Habakkuk 2:2

_____

_____

_____

_____

_____

_____

_____

_____

_____

_____

_____

Day 27

Today's Word:

Billionaire

Definition:

A person (possessing) assets worth at least a billion dollars

Declaration:

I am a "Billionaire"

I am a "Billionaire"

I am a "Billionaire"

I am a "Billionaire"

"Write the vision, and make it plain upon tables, that he may run that readeth it."

- Habakkuk 2:2

_____

_____

_____

_____

_____

_____

_____

_____

_____

_____

_____

_____

_____

Day 28

Today's Word:

Phenomenal

Definition:

Very remarkable extraordinary

Declaration:

I am "Phenomenal"

I am "Phenomenal"

I am "Phenomenal"

I am "Phenomenal"

"Write the vision, and make it plain upon tables, that he may run that readeth it."

- Habakkuk 2:2

Day 29

Today's Word:

Attracting

Definition:

The action or power of evoking interest, pleasure, or liking for someone or something

Declaration:

I am "Attracting"

I am "Attracting"

I am "Attracting"

I am "Attracting"

"Write the vision, and make it plain upon tables, that he may run that readeth it."

- Habakkuk 2:2

_____

_____

_____

_____

_____

_____

_____

_____

_____

_____

_____

_____

Day 30

Today's Word:

Blessed

Definition:

Highly favored or fortunate

Declaration:

I am "Blessed"

I am "Blessed"

I am "Blessed"

I am "Blessed"

*"Write the vision, and make it plain upon tables,
that he may run that readeth it."*

- Habakkuk 2:2

_____

_____

_____

_____

_____

_____

_____

_____

_____

_____

_____

_____

You can become an **AUTHOR** too!
Let us bring your book to **LIFE!**

www.GoClaxco.com

www.ingramcontent.com/pod-product-compliance
Lightning Source LLC
Chambersburg PA
CBHW070950180426
43194CB00041B/2023